How A Few Words Can Change Your Life

Brian B. Kim

Also by
Brian B. Kim:

Stock Market IQ & EQ:
The Vital, Fun, and
Concisely Definitive Introduction to Investing

Trading Stocks Using Classical Chart Patterns:
A Complete Tactical & Psychological Guide
for Beginners and Experienced Traders

For C.

Contents

A short saying often contains much wisdom.

Sophocles

Chapter 1
Which Words?

A man should read as his fancy takes him, for
what he reads as a chore will do him little good.

Samuel Johnson

Books are good enough in their own way,
but they are a mighty bloodless substitute for living.

Robert Louis Stevenson

It is what you read when you don't have to
that determines what you will be when you can't help it.

Oscar Wilde

This book is for you if:

- You hate books

or

- You think everything you are "supposed" to read is boring and everything you want to read does not seem important enough.

My message is simple: read anything that you have any interest in. And "anything" really means anything, including:

- Quotes
- Comic strips
- Cereal boxes
- Food labels
- Advertisements
- Slogans
- Short essays
- A paragraph
- A two-sentence paragraph
- A sentence
- A phrase
- Movies
- Tweets
- Magazines
- Anything with words
- Anything that people say is not "serious" reading
- Even books (if you want to)

Everything on this list can lead to life-changing perspective and knowledge. Each chapter in this book will take words from different places like a quote, movie, or cereal box and show you that there is no limit to the ideas you can learn and the places you can go with a few words.

Part of the reason we don't read more or at all is that we assume reading means reading a "serious" book. But books can be thick or boring or both. Even if a 500-page book contains priceless insights that will make you a better person, you will not benefit if you stop reading after three pages or don't open the book at all. Even if you finish the book, you might not understand it. Don't get me wrong: there is nothing wrong with reading a book. The problem is thinking that books are the only source of wisdom and the only way to do "good" or "serious" reading. Another problem is not being more gutsy when reading. We should be open to both trying something new and also putting it down if it does not grab our attention. Life-changing and fun ideas are everywhere, so you should not dwell on something that does not inspire you.

That said, remember that words can only teach or remind us that we can be decent and wise. Our actions, not the number of words we read, determine our character. Still, reading is a great way to recharge our minds, reaffirm life, get new ideas, and remind ourselves of timeless truths. The most important thing is that we read whatever interests us—and I do mean *whatever*. We will do more harm than good if we force ourselves to read a book we have no interest in just because the book is a "classic" that every "smart" person must read.

Now, let's find out what's out there and see how a few words can lead us from low spirits to serendipity and a new world.

Chapter 2
Embarrassing Words

Our lives are defined by fear more than we realize.

Anonymous comment on a blog

To show you that I am serious about reading anything, here is a quote from the October 2012 issue of *O, The Oprah* magazine:

> . . . how one simple piece of advice can make all the difference. The right words at the right time can set you on a new path, open your eyes to something you hadn't considered . . . . Whenever I encounter a flash of wisdom, I feel invigorated, refreshed . . . .

Yes, I am a guy and I have read *The Oprah Magazine*. But are these words not true? Haven't you felt shockingly rejuvenated and excited by a few words? Didn't the words seem to rescue you at just the right time?

So how did I end up reading *The Oprah Magazine*? I stopped by a snack shop at a public library and I noticed Ms. Winfrey's magazine on a table, lost and perhaps about to be thrown away.

I flipped through the issue and found the words above that will give me an encouraging nudge every time I read or remember them. Life is tough, and every break and serendipity helps.

Rather than waiting for good fortune, you can get lucky more often by keeping a notebook. I don't call it a diary because then we get the idea that we need to fill the pages with perfect sentences about only "important" things. So we should call our notebook a scribble book. We don't have to use complete sentences. I write mostly lists and phrases.

My scribbles include quotes, things I did, people I met, and ideas that I just want to get down. I also write down song names and pleasant or sad experiences with a short description. I often include the day's weather. Every time I flip through my scribble book months or years later, I am glad that I took the several seconds to jot down my thoughts. When I am outside, I use a simple note-taking program on my phone and then later copy my thoughts down using a pencil. Do whatever works for you. Fancy equipment is not required. Reviewing observations that didn't seem special at the time can be life-affirming moments when our spirits are down.

Am I exaggerating the importance of mere moments of encouragement? Here's a line from Thomas Hardy's novel *Far From the Madding Crowd* :

> Men thin away to insignificance and oblivion . . . when
> they [lack] good spirits when they are indispensable.

Then why not turn to words that remind and encourage us as often as we need and want them? One of the themes of this book is that you should decide what's important to you. If you feel you get something out of a few words, then you should feel very lucky and not be embarrassed to return to them often.

The writer Eric Hoffer also talked about the importance of those moments when we are at our best:

> That which is **unique and worthwhile** in us makes itself felt only in **flashes**. If we do not know how to catch and savor the flashes we are without growth and without exhilaration. (emphasis added)

And when these exhilarating flashes inevitably leave you, you should never be embarrassed about turning to "obvious" words for help. Again, aren't we so lucky to be able to change our mood with just a few words?

Also, realize that we forget so easily, including and especially the "obvious" truths. We know right from wrong. We know we should be grateful. We know effort matters. And at times we keep these truths at the top of our minds for a while, perhaps hours or even days. Then we forget and descend into whining and darkness. Words jotted down in a notebook can never prevent our regular trips to the darkness. But words can reduce the severity of our stumbles. Words can even speed up our return to something closer to our best selves. We need continuous reminders of obvious truths.

By the way, you should be excited whenever you are embarrassed. I have found that:

> the more we find something embarrassing, the more likely that we have found something important to us that we should pursue and hold onto.

When we are touched deeply by something, we worry about how friends, family, and strangers will judge us. Are we enjoying something that others disapprove of? Are we enjoying something "weird" or "not serious"? We are afraid to reveal what touches our hearts out of fear of being embarrassed and mocked. We want to avoid the awkwardness of revealing who we are and what we hold most important only to find others ridiculing us. The fear of embarrassment makes us avoid what we want to do. We seek safety and approval. But here's the thing: you don't have to tell anyone what you like. We can protect what is most important to us in the privacy of our mind. There is a time for friends and sharing. And there is a time for pursuing your own interests.

We shouldn't dismiss how the fear of social embarrassment affects our lives. Let me give you a not-so-serious but telling example. I like to drive listening to music with my windows down. One of my favorite songs is a 1980s pop hit by a female singer. So I'm stopped at a red light listening to the song and a car pulls up. My windows are down and I know the other driver can hear the song. I like to think that I am an independent and mature person, and so I keep listening to the song without turning down the volume. Even so, I'm sort of worried what the other driver, especially if the driver is a man, thinks about my music taste. I'm worried that I'm listening to a song that a guy should not enjoy. So sometimes I change the song or turn down the volume.

If others' expectations can make us change the song we are listening to in our car, then how else can society pressure us? By telling us to read only certain kinds of books? Pushing us to work in a job we don't like? Pressuring us to wear certain clothes and be someone we are not? These are serious stuff. We need all the help we can get to fight social pressure. And if simple reminders of timeless truths help us, then we must overcome our fear of embarrassment and use what we find useful.

By the way, since this book is about reading things that you like rather than things that you *should* like, let me stress that just because I refer to a book or anything else does not mean you should read it too. If you want to try it, go for it. If you find it boring, then toss it. The key is to follow your interests and instincts. For example, some people dismiss self-help books as shallow. But if you are curious, you might become interested after reading a random page. That's what happened to me with Dale Carnegie's *How to Stop Worrying & Start Living* where I found one of the most obvious and important sentences that I have read:

> If you were to read everything that has ever been written about worry by the great scholars of all time, you would never read anything more basic or more profound than such hackneyed proverbs as "Don't cross your bridges until you come to them" and "Don't cry over spilt milk." **If we only applied those two proverbs—instead of snorting at them**—we wouldn't need this book at all. In fact, **if we applied most of the old [and cheesy] proverbs, we would lead almost perfect lives**. (emphasis added)

We know that we shouldn't worry about problems until they arrive—if they come at all ("Don't cross your bridges until you come to them"). We know also that we should not waste our time worrying about the past. But do we follow these truths? Knowing something is one thing. Using our knowledge to improve ourselves is something else. We fail to apply what we know much of the time. Our failure is partly due to stubbornness. Even if we remember something, we ignore it because of laziness or arrogance. Our failure is also because of our incredible forgetfulness. So the goal is to make some essential lessons easier to remember. And few things are as memorable as a good movie. We'll talk about movies next.

Chapter 3
Movies

Not bad . . . for a human.

The synthetic human Bishop in the movie *Aliens*

Does watching a movie count as reading? Why not, especially if even a single line in a film takes us somewhere new. Also, we can read what others have written about a movie and pick up something we missed.

Here are some of my favorite movies:

- *Casablanca* (1942)
- *The Searchers* (1956)
- *Empire Strikes Back* (1980)
- *Back to the Future* (1985)
- *Aliens* (1986)
- *Ferris Bueller's Day Off* (1986)
- *Contact* (1997)
- *Casino Royale* (2006)

I like *Ferris Bueller's Day Off* because it takes me back to my senior year in high school. It also had a memorable line: "Life moves pretty fast. If you don't stop and look around for a while, you could miss it." Which is true. I like *The Searchers* because of the last scene where John Wayne's character turns around and walks away. That's not the only part I like but that's the part that makes the movie special to me. We don't need a reason to like a movie. And a movie doesn't have to teach an important life lesson. But every movie can be looked at in an interesting way.

Take *Aliens* from my list. If you have not seen it, *Aliens* is a science-fiction action film with some elements of horror that shows a lot of fighting between humans and alien monsters. I hate horror films because I find them scary, stupid, and frustrating.

So I should hate *Aliens*. Yet I find *Aliens* compelling. The movie's characters (human, alien, and artificial intelligence), sarcastic yet touching humor, and portrayal of hope and greed always stayed with me. The special effects still look fantastic. *Aliens*, like all good art, is timeless—or, it is to me at least. But just how meaningful and deep could a 1986 sci-fi action movie featuring an alien queen monster that lays its eggs inside live humans be? I doubted others thought the movie was important in any way. Still, I always felt there was something special about *Aliens*.

About two years ago, I read on the web Tim Carmody's essay "Why James Cameron's *Aliens* is the Best Movie About Technology." Carmody writes that *Aliens* is not just "fun" but also has big ideas, especially "a deep message about human beings and their relationship to technology." Then Carmody addressed the objection—the same doubt I had—that, sure, *Aliens* is fun but not "high art." That is, the movie is entertaining but not deep and important. Wrong. He says that *Aliens* is both fun and deep. So, I was not alone in thinking that there is something special about *Aliens*.

Of course Carmody has put into words what I only felt. By the way, finding out that we are not alone is one of the best things about reading. When we know that there is a similar or sympathetic mind out there, we are encouraged to continue to pursue what we like. Maybe we are not so weird to like a particular book, movie, cereal, ice cream flavor, or cartoon? Maybe we are not alone in feeling a certain way? Maybe we also can write words that will ease another's loneliness?

So what is Carmody's argument? In the final scenes of *Aliens*, Ellen Ripley, the main character played by actress Sigourney Weaver, is in a climactic fight with the alien queen monster. This alien species is impressive: it is born with advanced weapons technology built into its body. Its bone and skin can cut metal. Its limbs and double jaws can rip apart a human. Its acid blood can kill us.

In contrast, humans are born naked. On our own, we struggle to survive against not just this alien species but things like cold weather and maybe even a few coyotes. So we use technology. We build machines and weapons. Technology makes us powerful and improves our lives. Yet Carmody argues that what makes us truly human is not our ability to develop and use technology but our ability to "stand apart from the things we've made" by "set[ting] them aside" when appropriate. We know sometimes to "let . . . go [of our tools.]"

The importance of letting go of our gadgets is shown in the final battle. Ripley is wearing a robotic suit used to lift heavy objects. The mechanical power boost of the suit allows Ripley to throw the monster down an airlock tunnel and try to expel the monster out of the spaceship. But she tumbles down the airlock with the monster. Fortunately, the alien is pinned beneath Ripley's robotic suit. Crucially, Ripley unbuckles herself from the power-loader suit and starts climbing out of the airlock. She opens the airlock door and the alien is about to sucked out to space. But the monster grabs Ripley's foot. As Ripley hangs on for her life, she is saved when her shoe—another piece of technology—slips off her foot and is sucked out to space with the alien.

The point is that both the power-loader robotic suit and shoe, while useful technologies, are not ultimately us. We can use them to our benefit but we can also set them aside. Even when we put our gadgets down, we do not lose the essence of who we are as humans. In contrast, the queen alien cannot wiggle out of her armored skin when she is pinned down because her armor and weapons are built into her. Technology of the most advanced kind is the queen's downfall.

Did James Cameron, who wrote and directed *Aliens*, intend the movie to be interpreted as Carmody has? I don't know. Even if James Cameron had nothing or something else in mind when writing the movie, that does not mean Carmody's argument is worthless. At the least, it is interesting. When I started to read movie reviews in high school, I liked how the most interesting reviews had a fascinating argument about a larger meaning to the movie. Whether the movie creators intended that meaning is a fair question but not the most important. If we get enjoyment or new perspective out of a movie, then that is most important regardless of the "real" intent of the movie.

Whether or not you agree with Carmody, you can evaluate the idea that while technology is useful and often life-saving, it is not who we are—that in some ways, we might be better off without so much technology. While I do not want to return to a time when we lacked life-saving antibiotics or washed our clothes by hand, I think we expect sometimes too much from our gadgets. There is something about electronic gadgets that seem to promise permanent enlightenment, happiness, and progress. But just how essential, say, is the Internet to our lives? If you must choose between something as boring and old-technology as indoor plumbing (including the flush toilet) versus the Internet, which technology would you choose? I choose indoor plumbing and not having to use a hole in the ground as the restroom. It's not that the Internet isn't useful or hasn't improved my life. But I can do without it. So can you.

When it comes to truly foundational things like gaining wisdom and perspective, the Internet is not necessary. After all, there are public libraries and words on paper. Consider the following observation:

> *The Young Man's Best Companion, The Farrier's Sure Guide, The Veterinary Surgeon, Paradise Lost, The Pilgrim's Progress, Robinson Crusoe, Ash's Dictionary,* and *Walkingame's Arithmetic,* constituted his library; and though a limited series, it was one from which he had **acquired more sound information by diligent perusal** than many a man of opportunities has done from **yards of laden shelves**. (emphasis added)

Eight books made up the personal library of Gabriel Oak, one of the main characters in Thomas Hardy's *Far From the Madding Crowd*.

And eight books, perhaps even three or four, can be enough. Four books won't tell us everything about the world, but four good books that we enjoy can guide us to a meaningful life. This simplicity should comfort us as it says wisdom is accessible and does not require a mansion full of expensive books. What makes the difference is continuously reminding ourselves of essential truths through review.

The more I read, the more I feel that a small number of words can do so much for us. The amazing happens when we just start, whether with an essay or just a paragraph. We realize that a couple of sentences can give us new perspective. We learn that we need not know everything not just because that is impossible but because there are only a handful of essential truths that matter. We also gain the confidence to be patient. The nugget we picked up today will carry us through until we are ready to explore a new thing of our choosing.

Chapter 4
Graduation Speeches

There is no better measure of a person
than what he does when he is absolutely free to choose.

Wilma Askinas

You may have heard about or read Steve Job's graduation speech at Stanford in 2005. It is to-the-point and inspiring. But I think another graduation speech from 2005 is just as interesting and ultimately more important. Let's start with Jobs's speech.

Jobs said that "[you] must trust that" your experiences will "somehow connect in your future. You have to trust in something—your gut, destiny, life, karma, whatever." He also talked about getting fired from Apple, the company he started with Steve Wozniak. Jobs says that getting fired was the best thing because afterwards he met his wife and worked on ideas and technologies that led to future successes when he returned to Apple.

Jobs' discussion of death was most interesting to me. Jobs was diagnosed with cancer in 2003 and died in 2011. He said:

Remembering that I'll be dead soon is the most important tool I've ever encountered to help me make the big choices in life. Because almost everything—**all external expectations, all pride, all fear of embarrassment or failure—these things just fall away in the face of death, leaving only what is truly important.** Remembering that you are going to die is the best way I know to avoid the trap of thinking you have something to lose. You are already naked. **There is no reason not to follow your heart.** (emphasis added)

Despite the inevitability of death, Jobs's message is one of idealism and hope—an urgent call to seize your limited time. It is hard not to get a shot of energy from Jobs's words.

But the reality is that the most optimistic and idealistic among us will not be optimistic and idealistic every hour of every day. All of us regularly lethargic and uninspired. Remember Eric Hoffer's statement that:

That which is **unique and worthwhile** in us makes itself felt **only in flashes**. (emphasis added)

What do we in the meanwhile, between the flashes of inspiration? One might say that life is a series of meanwhiles filled with doubt, boredom, and drudgery broken by shorter periods of energy. Steve Jobs's speech can inspire us during our best moments to reach even higher. The speech may also inspire us during dull moments. But I think we need a different approach for the challenges and frustrations of everyday life.

Another way to make the best of daily life is the topic of David Foster Wallace's graduation speech at Kenyon College in 2005. Wallace was one of the most famous writers of the last 30 years. That doesn't mean we have to read his books. His Kenyon speech contains much to think about, and you may decide that the speech is sufficient.

Wallace said that "the most obvious . . . important realities are often the ones that are the hardest to see and talk about." This statement, he admits, is "just a banal platitude"—a boring and obvious statement. He continues: "but the fact is that, in the **day-to-day trenches of adult existence, banal platitudes can have life-or-death importance**." (emphasis added) In short, some boring and obvious words can save your life.

Wallace continued his speech by saying that education, at its best, teaches us "how to think." Another boring and obvious statement, Wallace admits, but Wallace explains:

> 'Learning how to think' really means learning how to exercise some control over how and why you think. It means being conscious and aware enough to **choose what you pay attention to** and to **choose how you construct meaning from experience**. Because if you cannot **exercise this kind of choice** in adult life, you will be **totally hosed**. (emphasis added)

By "totally hosed" Wallace doesn't mean annoyed or unhappy. He means frustration or depression so crushing as to lead to great suffering and perhaps suicide. Wallace warns us, and we should know from our own lives, that our minds can cause brutal inner torment if we fail to control what and how we think. Wallace pointed out:

> It is not the least bit coincidental that adults who commit suicide with firearms almost always shoot themselves in the head.

Even if you find this discussion gruesome, you should think about Wallace's words. Life is difficult but worth fighting for, and we might benefit from the advice of someone like Wallace who suffered from depression and wanted to help others deal with life's difficulties.

What does it mean to choose how we interpret our experiences? Let's talk about day-to-day life. Everyday life is often uninspiring. We know this.

Or do we?

If we knew the challenges of everyday reality, then we might talk about them more. Wallace said:

> **[Y]ou graduating seniors do not yet have any clue what 'day in, day out' really means**. There happen to be whole large parts of adult American life that nobody talks about in commencement speeches. One such part involves **boredom, routine, and petty frustration**. (emphasis added)

Wallace asks us to imagine ourselves at the supermarket after a tiring day at work. We're hungry. We just want to pick up some dinner before going to bed. But there are so many things that get in our way: traffic, crowded market, kids, old people who block your shopping cart, long checkout lines, and getting cut off by people driving military SUVs that get five miles per gallon. However,

petty, frustrating crap like this is exactly where the work of choosing comes in. (emphasis added)

Because if we:

"don't make a conscious decision about how to think and what to pay attention to, [we're] going to be pissed and miserable every time [we shop and go about daily life]."

So how can we think differently about this everyday scene at the market?

Instead of focusing on your tiredness, you can think about how there are probably many people in line who have lives that are much "harder, more tedious or painful" than yours. You can even think warmly and graciously about the person driving the giant SUV who cut you off. How? Maybe the Hummer is "driven by a father whose little child is hurt or sick in the seat next to him, and he's trying to rush to the hospital, and he's in a way bigger, more legitimate hurry than I am—it is actually *I* who am in his way." And by thinking about and choosing the meaning of an experience, we have:

within [our] power to experience a crowded, loud, slow, **consumer-hell type situation as not only meaningful but sacred**, on fire with the same force that lit the stars—compassion, love, the sub-surface unity of all things. Not that that mystical stuff's necessarily true: The only thing that's capital-T True is that **you get to *decide* how you're going to try to see it**. (emphasis added)

In other words, Wallace is asking us to try to see the best in a situation. Let's return to the long line at the market. We spot someone cutting in line. He seems to be smirking. We are enraged. Is there any way to see this situation differently? Let's try. What if the line-cutter was abandoned by his parents when he was 10 years old and grew up with cold-hearted foster parents? What if the person is in a desperate hurry to get medicine to his kid? What if the person didn't cut in line at all? What if everybody allowed the person to go ahead? What if somebody was saving his spot? What if he just didn't have as many advantages growing up as we did?

Remember, we don't know if any of these possibilities are true. *But regardless of the truth, we can decide to see the situation in a different and more sympathetic way.* In the end, the question becomes: am I truly harmed by someone cutting in line? The answer is no. And so we can choose understanding, forgiveness, and perspective. In other words, according to Wallace:

You get to decide what to worship.

Do we worship forgiveness and understanding? Or do we worship getting the best in every situation and taking advantage of others? Just because we don't go to church does not mean we do not worship. Wallace says the "only choice we get is *what* we worship." And "an outstanding reason for choosing some sort of God or spiritual-type thing to worship . . . is that pretty much anything else will eat you alive." Here's why:

- If we worship money, then we will never have enough.
- If we worship our body and sex appeal, then we will always feel ugly.
- If we worship power, then we will feel weak and afraid.
- If we worship being seen as smart, then we will feel stupid and fear being exposed as a fraud.

Of course, as we said and as Wallace says, "we all know this stuff already—it's been codified as . . . proverbs, clichés, . . . [and] parables . . . [in] every great [moral] story." But Wallace says:

> The trick is keeping the truth up-front in daily consciousness.

We know but we forget, so we must remind ourselves—by keeping a scribble book, re-reading that quote or passage, and doing whatever that refills our memory.

Let's apply Wallace's thinking to other situations:

- If our preferred political candidate loses the election, then instead of becoming angry we can choose to think how other voters' preferences are just as legitimate as ours.

- If someone spills coffee on us, then instead of becoming angry we could think about how we would want others to forgive us if we spilled coffee on them. We might even be thankful that we have the time to be hanging out at a coffee shop and the money to buy overpriced coffee.

- If we fail and are going nowhere in our lives, then instead of becoming bitter we could be grateful that we have the freedom to try and fail and yet try again.

All this is not to say that Steve Jobs's speech is inferior to Wallace's speech. We are inspired when Jobs urges us to never stop looking for our passion. But between inspiring moments are stretches of everyday life, the dull in-betweens everyone must deal with. Inspiration is exhilarating, but not enough. Inspiration can shrivel amid everyday pettiness and frustrations. And for everyday living, Wallace's somber yet humane words are more important. Wallace shows us that we always have a choice, that we can choose to see even the most infuriating situation in a good or at least more sympathetic way.

Chapter 5
What Should I Do With My Life?

The biggest mistake people make in life
is not trying to make a living doing what they most enjoy.

Malcolm Forbes

Vocations which we wanted to pursue, but didn't,
bleed, like colors, on the whole of our existence.

Honoré de Balzac

Here are some things you might have heard about money:

- Once we make a certain amount, and this amount is much less than we think, more money doesn't make us happier.
- If we worship money, then we'll always be grasping for more.
- Money cannot buy love and friendship—at least not the real kind.

These things are true according to people who should know,

including our grandparents, the wisest thinkers in history, and people reflecting on their lives as they face death—and who could be more honest than people who are about to die? But we are human, and so we believe the "old" rules don't apply to us. Fine. Let's assume that money can bring happiness and that it is the best measure of life success. Then what's the best way to become wealthy and successful? For Steve Jobs, success is about following your passion. Let's look at some other opinions on this subject.

Maybe We Should *Not* Pursue Our "Passion"

Scott Adams, the creator of the comic strip *Dilbert*, says:

> Passion is bullsh*t.

Adams's reasoning is simple: "It's easy to be passionate about things that are working out, and that distorts our impression of the importance of passion." If we were to put this in our own words:

Success causes passion more than passion causes success.

So Adams is a kind of anti-Steve Jobs when it comes to life advice. Adams says we should forget about looking for our passion. Instead, if we find something we're good at it (regardless of whether we like it at first), then we are likely to develop a passion for it.

Take window cleaning. Let's say we are good at using a squeegee. We seem to never miss a spot on a window and we clean all the dirt with one pass. Chances are we don't think much of this "skill." Window cleaning is certainly not prestigious (we'll discuss prestige later in this chapter). We couldn't make a living creating spotless windows. Or could we? Millions of people who own unglamorous businesses are far wealthier than many people with "prestigious" jobs. Put it this way: you might be motivated to become passionate about cleaning windows and unclogging drains if you are good at these things and can make a good living doing them.

Why are we talking about fixing pipes and cleaning windows? So that we don't ignore careers that we might be very good at even if we don't think we have a passion for them. So be open to trying new things and discovering what you are good at. There is dignity in all labor. Also remember what we said about embarrassment. If you fear getting embarrassed about something, then you probably found something that means something to you. Let others gossip while you walk your path.

Why Prestige is Dangerous

We hurt ourselves when we don't do something we like because we fear others will mock us. We also hurt ourselves when we do something not because we like it but because it is prestigious— because others approve it. But prestige is often a trap. Consider what technology investor Paul Graham says about prestige:

> Prestige is like a powerful magnet that warps even your beliefs about what you enjoy. It causes you to work not on what you like, but what you'd **like to like**. (emphasis added)

So we give up what we like to do and decide to do something more "prestigious" like being a doctor, accountant, consultant, or banker. There is nothing wrong with being a lawyer or doctor if you want to be a lawyer or doctor. But being a doctor because others think highly of medicine is the way to unhappiness.

How much risk should you take?

Some say that being unenthusiastic about your "safe" job is better than going on your own because there are risks to starting a business or pursuing writing, art, a hunch, or a passion. But there are also risks to a job that seems to pay a steady paycheck: lack of creative freedom, unpleasant bosses, little control over your time, office politics, and your indifference. Burnout and quitting are common, and there goes the safe paycheck.

I believe we must take some risk. Risk is unavoidable in life. Many have said that in life the riskiest thing to do is to not take any risk. Whenever I feel I am pursuing stability and comfort above all else, I try to remember the following quote by Hellen Keller:

Life is either a daring adventure, or nothing at all.

I'm not saying you should get a certain job or quit your job or even have a job. I'm saying that since life is risk, you might as well go for some things.

The next perspective on work and success can help us put together the different views in this chapter.

<u>Just Keep Doing Sometime You Like</u>

If we do something we enjoy long enough, we will become very good at it, and fame and wealth—if we desire them—will come naturally. This message is from Raj Raghunathan who was interviewed by Joe Pinsker for the April 2016 issue of *The Atlantic* magazine in an article titled "Why So Many Smart People Aren't Happy." Raghunathan says:

> When you **don't need to compare yourself to other people**, you gravitate towards things that you **instinctively enjoy** doing, and you're good at, and if you just focus on that for a **long enough time**, then **chances are very, very high** that you're going to progress towards **mastery** anyway, and the fame and the power and the money and everything will come as a byproduct, rather than something that you chase directly in trying to be superior to other people. (emphasis added)

I like this statement, and perhaps you identify with it as well. It acknowledges the fact that we are not going to be successful unless we enjoy our work. It also emphasizes our responsibility to keep working on what we like. Thus, it combines "passion," which can drift into the aimless superficiality, with hard work, which adds discipline and focus. Next, let's see what it might look like to mix effort and enthusiasm.

Working at a Grocery Store

In *Why I Quit My Full-Time Job to Work at Trader Joe's* (you can find the article at http://spoonuniversity.com/lifestyle/why-i-quit-my-full-time-job-to-work-at-trader-joes/), Katherine Baker writes about feeling lost and being unemployed after graduating from college. When she got an office job as a therapist, she hated it. One day she went to the grocery store and thought about working there because the place seemed fun. The store was Trader Joe's. Trader Joe's is a grocery chain with a devoted following. I know people who moved to live near a Trader Joe's.

Baker quit her therapist job and was getting ready to start her first day at Trader Joe's. But, she says:

> looming self-doubt crept up again in the back of my mind, and I thought, "Oh my gosh. I'm a 24-year-old college graduate and I'm working at a grocery store, while all my friends have jobs in finance and engineering or are in med school? I seriously suck at life."

So:

> . . . I almost didn't go to my first day of work

Why? Because she was comparing herself to her friends and she was embarrassed about working at a grocery store. Here is another reminder about how powerful the fear of embarrassment is. Fortunately for Katherine and us:

. . . I put my hesitations aside and started training. And slowly . . . I began to love my job. [B]efore I knew it, I was happy as sh*t.

. . .

I had aspirations again!

Also:

. . . I wasn't jealous of anyone's life anymore.

And:

I realized I need to chase things that matter to me, things I'm passionate about. I ended up finally coming to terms with the fact that I didn't want to go to med school, and that I wanted to pursue nutrition and food science (which I'm working on now), and I like to think that working at Trader Joe's helped me see the light and value in doing things that you enjoy.

One more thing:

Moreover, I learned there's absolutely no shame in working in a grocery store or anywhere for that matter . . . .

As we said, there is dignity in all labor. Baker says you must:

find the things in life that make you happy and unapologetically pursue them.

Becoming very good at something we find exciting is the best way to fulfillment, freedom, financial security, and all else. Remember that finding something you like is just a first step. You need to keep at it to achieve mastery. We have to combine our idealism and excitement with patience and persistence.

Chapter 6
Opposite Words

The line between failure and success is so fine
that we scarcely know when we pass it—
so fine that we often are on the line and do not know it.

Ralph Waldo Emerson

This chapter is about an obvious but infrequently-tried idea: when you are frustrated, stuck, bored, angry, hopeless, or looking for something new, you should try the opposite of what you've been doing.

One reason few of us try the opposite is because it is unpleasant to admit that we were on the wrong path. Another reason is that it simply does not occur to us to try all possible solutions to a problem. Trying the opposite is too "obvious" for us to notice. Yet another reason is that we don't want the opposite to work: it is embarrassing to realize that the answer was right next us. But this chapter is not about ridiculing our stubborn blindness. It is about flexibility and finding powerful possibilities by simply looking in places that we have not checked. It is about questioning our assumptions.

We discussed already one idea that overturns our assumptions. In Chapter 2, we said:

> The more we find something embarrassing, the more likely that we have found something important to us that we should pursue and hold onto.

This statement seems contradictory and counter-intuitive because we assume that our embarrassment indicates we did something wrong and therefore we should stop what we are doing. But what if we are embarrassed because we are afraid that others will mock the things we love? Then, as Ralph Waldo Emerson said, you must:

> Always do what you are afraid to do.

Let's look at two more counter-intuitive statements. The goal is to get us in the habit of reconsidering "obviously wrong" ideas. The ideas that we have discarded have a good chance of being just what we need.

Success Is Not What It Seems

The next counter-intuitive statement is from the book *The Secrets of Consulting* by Gerald M. Weinberg:

> Past glories are future graves.

How can we be led to failure by our past accomplishments? Let's say that after much hard work, we became successful. Now we want to relax a bit. After all, work is hard. Work is hard not just because it is work but also because it is unpredictable. Work involves not just physical labor but mental discomfort from anxiety and worry due to the fact that there are no guarantees in life no matter how hard you work. So we stop and enjoy thinking about our accomplishments. But when we stop, we start to decline.

Unfortunately, there is competition. Other students want to do better than you, competitors want to steal your clients, and the economy can crash and ruin your business. Competition means we can't stop. But we desperately want to rest on our past glories and wish away the competition. We stop moving forward and our success starts to rot. Thus, isn't it reasonable to say:

Success is failure.

Is it ridiculous to say success if failure? Not really. If you think "success is failure" is too harsh, let's change it to:

Success is failure if we don't continue forward.

But since humans are always looking for the easy way, we will rely on past victories and stop moving forward. So we are back to:

Success is failure.

No matter how meaningful a success, we need to do other things if we don't want our lives to be defined by one thing.

Let's now consider the opposite:

Failure is success.

Is this more ridiculous?

Take two people who are standing on Point A. Their goal is to reach Point B. The first person just graduated from college with honors and is proud of his academic accomplishments. The second person did not go to college and is starting a plumbing business.

The first person feels on top of the world. He feels his college degree allows him to relax. He is relying on his past success to get to Point B.

The second person dropped out twice from a plumbing apprenticeship program but eventually earned his plumbing license. The plumber did not find any work for six months, but since then has steadily found more work. In other words, the second person has failed several times but has always moved forward.

Isn't the plumber closer to success (Point B) despite his repeated failures merely by not staying still at Point A like the college graduate? Whenever we are working toward something, we are closer to our goal and farther away from failure (standing still) than a person who tries to make a previous, temporary success into a permanent success. So then:

Failure is success if we don't quit.

And that is exactly what Winston Churchill said:

Success consists of going from failure to failure without loss of enthusiasm.

So all we have to do is keep going. But we don't. Why? We'll discuss that next.

<u>We Mistakenly Think We Have To Be Perfect</u>

One reason we don't keep moving forward is because we think failing once makes our life a permanent failure. This misunderstanding is understandable. Since we think success is permanent, we think failure is forever as well. But consider another seemingly ridiculous quote by Gerald Weinberg:

The business of life is too important to be taken seriously.

Many ideas are stuffed into this short and wonderful quote. Let's unpack it in our own words:

Life is precious. There is a good chance that Earth is the only place in the universe with life.

Everyone makes mistakes.

If we take our mistakes too seriously, then we can't move on. Not moving on means quitting life.

It is ridiculous to throw away something so precious as life just because of mistakes.

Laughing at our mistakes allows us to move on and embrace life.

The ability to laugh at ourselves is a very underrated quality. There are few things more sad than being unable to laugh at yourself. And the *inability to accept failure cripples us because that means we won't try anything if there is any possibility of failure.* As many have said:

Fear of failure guarantees failure.

Fear makes us timid and we try half-heartedly, which leads to failure. Fear can also stop us from trying at all, which is the worst thing. Shakespeare said:

Our doubts are traitors, and make us lose the good we oft might win, by fearing to attempt.

We can overcome our fear of failure by reminding ourselves that:

Repeated failure is the best way to succeed.

Because:

Having never failed makes you a failure.

Always re-examine your assumptions and never overlook "obvious" things.

Chapter 7
Shakespeare

A man that will enjoy a quiet conscience
must lead a quiet life.

Lord Chesterfield

Shakespeare?

Isn't this book about finding wisdom in places other than Shakespeare's plays and other so-called serious works? So why should we read them? Well, we might like one or two of the classics. Some people say that Shakespeare is the greatest writer ever in the English language and perhaps the greatest writer in any language.

We have a dilemma. We should read what we find interesting rather than what others say we should. And we should be extra wary about feeling obligated to read the so-called great books. Still, we might be curious about perhaps the most famous writer in history. So let's give Shakespeare a chance.

Let's do something that is consistent with this book's message: let's read something that is easy to understand and provides insights. Instead of tackling a Shakespeare play on our own, let's read an essay that discusses it. We are much less likely to give up. Even if we read a Shakespeare play by ourselves, there is a good chance we will miss Shakespeare's insights. So an essay that translates the difficult into digestible pieces is very useful.

Some might say that reading an essay about a play is not the same thing as reading the play itself. So what? What good is reading something if we don't understand it? It is infinitely better to read a short explanation of a book and therefore understand the main point rather than read the book and come away with nothing. Remember that we are reading to learn and not to be able to tell others that we read an important book.

We'll begin our Shakespeare journey with an essay titled "Why Shakespeare Is For All Time" by Theodore Dalrymple in the Winter 2003 issue of *City Journal* magazine. Before we start, let's talk briefly about "great" literature. If any work deserves to be called great, its merit should rest on its ability to give us deeper insights into timeless human issues such as greed, love, vanity, fear, anger, anxiety, and ambition—and does so in a generous spirit that makes the message understandable to all those who seek it.

At the beginning of his essay, Dalrymple quotes the following lines from Shakespeare's *Macbeth* where the main character Macbeth asks a doctor:

> Canst thou not minister to a
> mind diseased
> Pluck from the memory a rooted sorrow
> Raze out the written troubles
> of the brain

And with some sweet
oblivious antidote
Cleanse the stuffed bosom
of that perilous stuff
Which weighs upon the heart?

To this plea for help, the doctor has just a few words to say:

Therein the patient
Must minister to himself.

Macbeth has murdered the king and taken the throne. Macbeth commits more crimes. He is tormented by guilt, fear, paranoia, and regret. So Macbeth asks the doctor for help. The doctor says there is nothing he can do for Macbeth.

Let's translate this dialogue into our own words. The left side is the original text. The right side is my bad translation:

1 Canst thou not minister to a	1 Can you help
2 mind diseased	2 a suffering person
3 Pluck from the memory a rooted sorrow	3 By erasing sad memories
4 Raze out the written troubles	4 Getting rid of what bothers
5 of the brain	5 the mind
6 And with some sweet	6 With some
7 oblivious antidote	7 medicine

8 Cleanse the stuffed bosom	8 Wipe away from us
9 of that perilous stuff	9 Those bad feelings
10 Which weighs upon the heart?	10 That break our heart?

Let's simplify further Macbeth's lines:

> Hey doctor:
> Give me a pill that
> wipes away my worries,
> regrets, anxieties, and pain.

And now the doctor in our own words:

> Sorry, there is no such pill.
> We are on our own
> when it comes to
> finding peace.

Macbeth's doctor is not alone in saying this. For example, Ralph Waldo Emerson said:

> A political victory, a rise in the rents, the recovery of your sick, the return of your absent friend, or some other quite external event, raises your spirits, and you think good days are preparing for you. Do not believe it. **Nothing can bring you peace but yourself.** (emphasis added)

Emerson said it about 150 years ago. Shakespeare in *Macbeth* 400 years ago. And others thousands of years ago. There is nothing new under the sun. The important thing is remembering and applying the wisdom.

Let's return to the dialogue between Macbeth and the doctor. When the doctor tells Macbeth that there is no medicine that can eliminate our worries, heart aches, guilty conscience, anxieties, and whatever else that disturbs us because of our ambition or misdeeds, we can hear Macbeth's—and our—disappointment. Yes, our friends and family can comfort us. And yes, there is medicine to help people with real mental illnesses. But ultimately, we are on our own if we want peace of mind. And when we cross some lines—for example, by committing murder as Macbeth did—nothing can erase the guilt from our conscience. Some lines simply must not be crossed.

It is a sobering message, and its simplicity magnifies an unforgiving truth: some actions destroy our soul and humanity. Dalrymple writes:

> . . . Shakespeare destroys the utopian illusion that social arrangements [such as politics or medicine] can be made so perfect that men will no longer have to strive to be good. Original sin—that is to say, the sin of having been born with human nature that contains within it the **temptation to evil**—will always make a mockery of attempts at perfection [or quick fixes] based upon manipulation of the environment . . . .

And:

The **prevention of evil** will always require more than desirable social arrangements: it will **forever require personal self-control and the conscious limitation of appetites**. (emphasis added)

Much of *Macbeth* is about self-control and how we lose our soul when we don't respect the line that separates humanity from hell. When that line is crossed, we put ourselves in a place from which there is no return. I once heard that:

An artist is judged for his best works, but our character is judged based on our worst actions.

It is harsh, but it also seems correct.

Chapter 8
Ignored Words

The strongest poison ever known
came from Caesar's laurel crown.

William Blake

The highest proof of virtue
is to possess boundless power without abusing it.

Thomas Macaulay

For much of American history, leadership positions in business, government, finance, and law and spots in elite colleges were filled mostly with Americans who were white, male, and Protestant. This system started to open up in the 1960s and 1970s and today smart and ambitious people from all backgrounds, especially those who do well in school, can get into top-ranked universities and join prestigious professions. That does not mean that American meritocracy is perfect. Let's discuss three issues.

Issue #1: Hard work or luck?

The first issue is the role of luck in a meritocracy. Luck? Doesn't a meritocracy reward hard work? A lot of times, yes, and I believe in doing your best. But what determines a person's willingness and ability to put in the effort? Studies suggest that the genes that we inherit from our parents affect not only our intelligence but also our motivation, confidence, and personality. Our parents do not determine entirely our fate, but they do influence us a lot. And what could be more random and uncontrollable than who our parents are? We can't pick our parents. I am not saying that we are not responsible for our actions. What I am saying is that some people have a head start because their parents are smart and conscientious and these traits were passed down to them. As you should know, life is unfair.

Some people have genes that increase their chances of being healthy and successful in modern society. Others who are not as blessed use the gifts they have. And we all have gifts. As for the least fortunate among us, private charities and government assistance step in. The amount of government help a society decides to give to the least fortunate is one of the main issues of politics—and we will not come to an agreement as to the proper scope of government here or ever. Some societies offer generous help to those who are unable or even unwilling to take care of themselves. Others are stricter and place greater responsibility on individuals who are less talented. There is no "right" answer. Some people think generous aid should be given to everybody. Some argue that even if talent and ambition are unevenly distributed at birth, too much help can lead to moral corruption.

Others support a generous social safety net given the role of luck in our lives. But those who emphasize individual responsibility say that the government's leveling the playing field often results in the abuse of power and the loss of freedom. And so on.

Our job is not to settle this issue but to understand that luck plays a role even in a "fair" system. And if luck plays a role, empathy for the unlucky seems appropriate.

Issue #2: What kind of merit does American meritocracy value?

The second issue is the merit that gets rewarded in America today. Elite schools and professions emphasize smarts and ambition as measured by grades, test scores, and diplomas. Here is what columnist David Brooks wrote in his 2004 *New York Times* essay "Stressed for Success?":

> You are being judged [by colleges] according to criteria that you would never use to judge another person and which will never again be applied to you once you leave higher ed[ucation].

I agree with Brooks that colleges overemphasize "numbers" and superficial well-roundedness over traits like conscientiousness and creativity. I disagree with Brooks in that I think large parts of society continue to overemphasize things like test scores and school names well beyond college.

I don't have anything against good grades and ambition. The desire to excel drives achievement and innovation. But focusing on grades and credentials means overlooking things like honesty, empathy, and honor. While such virtues and a fancy degree are not mutually exclusive, emphasizing the importance of prestigious credentials does not guarantee that duty and a concern for others get adequate attention. We need to be reminded regularly about virtues that have nothing to do with grades and test scores. And this leads to the third issue.

Issue #3: "I earned my power and privilege"

The third issue is that we seem to have lost the desire to emphasize virtues such as public spiritedness and self-control as much as smarts and credentials. Here is Brooks in his 2012 *New York Times* essay "Why Our Elites Stink":

> The best of the [old White Anglo-Saxon Protestant] elites had a **stewardship mentality**, that they were temporary caretakers of institutions that would span generations. They cruelly ostracized people who did not live up to their codes of **gentlemanly conduct** and **scrupulosity**. They [had their faults], but they did believe in **restraint, reticence, and service**.

Here is columnist Ross Douthat in his 2011 *New York Times* essay "Our Reckless Meritocracy":

> For decades, the United States has been opening paths to privilege for its brightest and most determined young people, culling the best and brightest from Illinois and Mississippi and Montana and placing

them in positions of power in Manhattan and Washington. By elevating the children of farmers and janitors as well as lawyers and stockbrokers, we created what seems like the most capable, hardworking, high-I.Q. elite in all of human history.

Has all this brain power led to good policies and governance? Douthat says:

And for the last 10 years, we've watched this same elite lead us off a cliff—mostly by being too smart for its own good.

Why are some members of today's leadership class so reckless or selfish? A better question is why would any person in a position of power and privilege be immune from the temptations of power? We are human after all. The older elites were also ambitious and selfish. But they also had a stricter code of conduct to control their impulses. They stressed public service. They restrained their appetites. There were stiff social penalties for those who cut corners. This system seems to have worked better in some ways than whatever we have today. They seem to have agreed with Immanuel Kant that "out of the crooked timber of humanity, no straight thing was ever made," and therefore enforced strict rules of behavior. The older generations seem to have understood that we need continuous warnings about and social nudges against our fundamental selfishness.

In one sense, the current meritocracy is even more powerful and potentially dangerous than the old monarchies and aristocracies. Today's leaders have a "merit-based" justification for their power and privilege. After all, they did well in a competition based on school and credentials. They have less doubt about their fitness to make decisions that affect everyone because they feel their power is earned. Of course attending a highly selective school does not make someone a villain. But neither does it make the person exempt from permanent human weaknesses such as arrogance and selfishness. We seem to downplay this obvious point, if we think about it at all.

Empathy and Decency

So what can we do to fight the tendency to equate academic and professional credentials with virtue and civic-mindedness? One thing is to adopt a fair skepticism of experts and the super-credentialed. There are people who are brilliant and also wise and modest. But we should remember that brilliance does not equal virtue or even accuracy. Of course people with less education make mistakes too. The point is that all the education in the world cannot change the fact that we are human and prone to hubris, meanness, and evil.

Let me conclude with something George Orwell said in the 1940s about the English people:

> [They don't have] much admiration for great men. They have the virtues and vices of an old-fashioned people. To twentieth-century political theories [such as fascism and communism] they [don't] [pr]oppose [a] theory of their own, but a **moral quality which**

must be vaguely described as decency. (emphasis added)

I think there is an uplifting quality to citizens who, even if lacking in formal education, resist grand theories and do not defer automatically to the well-credentialed. You may find this stance too anti-intellectual. But education is useful only if we are also decent. If I must choose, I choose decency over intellect every time.

Chapter 9
Comic Strips

Pretty much all the honest storytelling there
is in the world is done by children.

Oliver Wendell Holmes

Let's talk about Charles Schulz's *Peanuts* comic strip. My favorite *Peanuts* characters are Linus with his blue blanket, Snoopy, and Schroeder. Everyone looks so peaceful. Even Lucy looks gentle when she is not screaming. I just find them endearing. Of course, I'm not alone in feeling this way. From the first *Peanuts* strip published on October 2, 1950 to the last on February 13, 2000, hundreds of millions of people have gotten happy feelings from some of the most popular fictional characters in history.

Peanuts has meant a lot to me since I watched a re-run of *A Charlie Brown Christmas* (1965) animated television show 30 years ago. But I did not read my first *Peanuts* strip until several years ago. All that time, I assumed that *Peanuts* was about happy kids playing happily in a happy All-American neighborhood. I could not have been more wrong about these kids.

But first, don't forget that we should enjoy and admire

something for our own reasons. We don't have to like something for the "right" reasons. I don't care if an art critic looks down on *Peanuts* as children's stuff. I think Schulz's work is brilliant in creating such deep and familiar emotions with breathtakingly few and clean lines.

I started my *Peanuts* investigation with the very first strip from October 2, 1950. My reaction? Confusion. These kids overflowed with sarcasm and treated each other badly. They were just mean.

In the first strip, two kids watch Charlie Brown coming down the sidewalk and one of them says: "How I hate him!"

(You can view every Peanuts strip at www.gocomics.com. The first strip is at www.gocomics.com/peanuts/1950/10/02, and from there you can go all the way to the last one.)

In the second strip, a girl punches Charlie Brown and gives him a black eye.

In the third strip, a girl casually steals a boy's umbrella during a rainstorm.

The fourth and fifth strips contain the quirky humor that I expected. So maybe the kids were just having bad days in the beginning.

But in the sixth *Peanuts* strip the kids are back to tormenting each other. A girl asks a boy:

"Will you still love me when you're grown up and are rich and famous, and I'm just a poor little girl?"

"Sure, I will . . ." the boy answers.

Then the boy asks the girl:

". . . And will you still love me if you get rich and famous and I don't have anything?"

The girl replies:

"That will be different!"

Funny, but also sad and even devastating. Because it is true. Not always, but often enough that this conversation might make us uncomfortable. But why are these kids talking like cynical adults? Perhaps I had forgotten how kids act. Maybe punching and stealing and breaking hearts are what children do. Also, haven't we all said or thought, "How I hate him!" to a classmate or a kid at the park for vague and imaginary reasons? Maybe we thought a kid looked at us funny. Maybe he was wearing a funny-looking shirt and we wanted him to know that we were better than him. We are superficial and cruel creatures after all. So perhaps *Peanuts* reflects our society as it is—with our selfishness, cruelty, and vanity—and Schulz made it easier for us to accept reality by using harmless and lovable messengers as carriers of some awful truths. Or maybe I was taking *Peanuts* too seriously. After all, it is just a comic strip.

Then in early 2016, I read the essay "The Exemplary Narcissism of Snoopy" by Sarah Boxer in *The Atlantic* magazine. Boxer writes:

Peanuts was deceptive. It looked like kids stuff, but it wasn't.

Boxer continues:

Many early *Peanuts* fans—and this may come as a shock to later fans [who were used to innocent storylines]—were attracted to the strip's decidedly **unsweet view of society**. (emphasis added)

What made *Peanuts* unique were ideas such as:

People, especially children, are selfish and cruel to one another; social life is perpetual conflict; solitude is the only peaceful harbor; one's deepest wishes will invariably be derailed and one's comforts whisked away; and an unbridgeable gulf yawns between one's fantasies about oneself and what others see. These bleak themes . . . floated freely on the pages of *Peanuts* . . . .

This combative interpretation may not be your view of *Peanuts*. Even if Charles Schulz's intent was to show how hard and disappointing life can be, that doesn't have to be what you take away from *Peanuts*. After all, aren't Snoopy and Charlie Brown's lovable faces on so many mugs, posters, sweaters, and airplanes selling countless products? The companies that pay tens of millions of dollars for the right to use the images of Snoopy and his friends to sell insurance, clothes, candies, vitamins, and everything else believe that shoppers think positively about *Peanuts*. Why does it matter if *Peanuts* was about the loneliness of life?

One answer is that it does not matter. But if we are curious, we might learn more about *Peanuts* creator Charles Schulz. For a couple of dollars, I bought a used copy of David Michaelis's excellent—and for me shockingly sad—biography of Charles Schulz titled *Schulz and Peanuts*. I thought how if anybody had reason to be fulfilled, surely it must be the person who created some of the most loved drawings and characters in history. My assumption was wrong. Michaelis writes the following about Schulz toward the end of Schulz's life:

> [In old age,] Schulz reminisced with [a friend], but all his memories seemed to be about being picked on as a boy, and about how he still wanted to meet the kids who had bullied him face-to-face and get even.

Then Michaelis quotes the friend:

> I'd always known that side of [Schulz]. But at a time when people usually resolve their unresolvable histories by making peace with the past, he was angry that he's never changed anything. You could see the bitterness in him . . . . Nothing in all of his seventy-seven years had been resolved.

And:

Schulz on his deathbed seemed "angry at God, angry with friends, angry with fate—angry [about] all the troubles he could never let go of."

I hesitated quoting these words because they might be seen as denigrating a person who has passed away. That is not my intention. Nobody resolves all of their regrets and demons. We all have insecurities and resentments. The point is that fame and money do not guarantee happiness or inner peace. This truth is captured by the following statement:

Be happy for no reason, or you will never be happy.

The irony is that *Peanuts* contains suggestions on how to face life's difficulties. Let's talk about them next.

<u>*Peanuts* as Life Strategies</u>

One way to look at Snoopy and the kids is that each character represents a different strategy against life's challenges:

- Charlie Brown is the luckless kid who is made fun of and does not get anything he wants. Yet Charlie Brown manages to be a loyal friend. He is patient and gives others the benefit of doubt. He seems decent no matter what. And he doesn't quit.

- Linus shields himself with his blanket against the unforgiving world. But Linus does not hide from life.

When problems confront him, he responds with calm and wisdom. While Linus is younger than others, he provides vital stability and perspective to his friends.

- Lucy is sarcastic and often mean. But Lucy's tough personality reflects vulnerability more than rudeness. Her demeanor is her shield against getting hurt. One way to avoid getting your heart broken is to boast and adopt a cool demeanor. Lucy's boasting stems from insecurity, but it also reflects courage. And guts is important because sometimes we need to make something out of nothing. Often something good results when we just go for it. Lucy reminds me of friends whose irrational confidence helps me get through difficult times. Their zesty attitude gives me courage just when I need it.

- Schroeder is always playing his toy piano. I don't know if Schroeder will become a famous concert pianist. I hope he makes it if he wants to be one. But it does not matter whether Schroeder becomes the best at the thing he loves, and the same principle applies to us. If you love writing, playing piano, drawing, cooking, running, or whatever, then you should not be embarrassed about enjoying it even if you are not the best. The thing that matters is that you get fun and meaning out of doing something at your level. Ignore the onlookers just as Schroeder does. I relate to Schroeder because I get much enjoyment from playing piano. I don't care how many millions of people in the world play the piano better than me because Schroeder doesn't either.

- Then there is Snoopy the beagle. True, Snoopy can't talk to the kids. But he doesn't need to because his love for life is based on his imagination. Snoopy imagines himself to be a World War I fighter pilot, a cool dude popular with ladies, a famous writer, and so on. Snoopy is in his own world, stubbornly content yet still lovable. You might say that Snoopy is in denial and that is not a good thing. But imagination is different from denial. Imagination helps us set goals and think new thoughts, and these things allow us to live better in the real world. Ironically, imagination allows us to see ourselves more clearly. Sometimes it is only in our imagination that who we really are can be shielded from the distorted judgments of society. It takes a fine balance of guts, self-awareness, and perspective to hold onto our values in the world, and Snoopy managed it. Maybe that's why we love dogs.

Peanuts as a Reminder that Life is Rough on Everyone

Besides suggesting _how_ we might deal with life's difficulties (Charlie Brown's decency, Linus's heroic calm, Lucy's courage-forming banter, Snoopy's imagination), I think Schulz has a second message that is more basic and important: everyone _will_ face difficulties. There are many ways to face life, but the first step is accepting the fact that there _will_ be challenges.

Is this message too obvious to have any value for adults? Is it useful for only kids like Charlie Brown, Lucy, and Linus who don't know what adults know? (Actually, I think the kids know already.) Before you dismiss it, remember how obvious ideas can be some of the most powerful ideas. Also, consider what psychologist Robert Maurer says about adults:

> Adults . . . **assume that if they are living correctly, they can control the events around them. When fear does appear, it seems all wrong . . . .** This approach to fear is unproductive. **If your expectation is that a well-run life should always be orderly, you are setting yourself up for panic and defeat.** If you assume that a new job or relationship or health goal is supposed to be easy, you will feel angry and confused when fear arises—and you'll do anything to make it disappear. (emphasis added)

Life spares no one, not adults and not even kids with heartbreaking smiles. We will experience tragedies. Others will make fun of our dreams and opinions. Someone will threaten us for driving slow. We will be disrespected, and we will disrespect others. This is life. If we deny this reality, we will fail.

Why did Schulz use a comic strip for this tough message? Sending a message through art—whether a writing, painting, movie, song, or comic strip—makes "obvious" truths memorable and unpleasant truths easier to accept. If a tough message is triple-coated with sugar in the form of strikingly harmless cartoon characters and hidden to the point of being invisible or misunderstood, then readers can think about it and accept it gradually.

Before we leave, let me discuss my favorite *Peanuts* strip. It is from November 5, 1972. Early November means autumn and crisp air. Charlie Brown and Peppermint Patty are taking a stroll on a fall day as leaves fall around them. Although autumn and colorful leaves come every year, there seems to be just a handful of fall days that are perfect when the sunlight is just right, the leaves are just the right color, and the air has just the right mystery—just as it is not every day that we are at our best. Peppermint Patty talks about the rareness of our best moments when she tells Charlie Brown:

> Life is like a bracelet . . . . It has little jewels around it which are like the little bright moments that come along in our lives every now and then . . . .

Then she asks Charlie Brown:

> Do you feel that way, Chuck? If you do, you should tell me.

Charlie Brown:

> Why yes . . . I think you're right . . . Life is very much like a collar.

Peppermint Patty:

> NOT A COLLAR, CHUCK. A BRACELET!!!

Haven't we all felt frustrated when others did not understand our deepest feelings? Like Peppermint Patty, we take a chance and open our hearts to someone and . . . disappointment.

Here's the thing. We like to think that we are important, and we are to our friends and family. But that does not mean the world revolves around us. Like Peppermint Peppy, I love taking walks on autumn days with the leaves falling around me. But when my friends did not seem to share my fondness for the leaves turning color, I felt annoyed, and special. Before you laugh at my self-centeredness, I think I have matured and have learned to enjoy moments on my own without needing others to confirm my insights about fall weather. This *Peanuts* strip reminds me of the importance of having the courage to enjoy what I like and also the humility to not impose my views on others. Whether or not others care about our feelings, I think Charlie Brown and Linus would suggest that we care about theirs.

Chapter 10
You Are Rich

The hardest arithmetic to master is that
which enables us to count our blessings.

Eric Hoffer

Rice and Water

Growing up, I attended sleepover camps at the YMCA where we
ate only rice and water for one meal. The camp counselors told
us that the purpose was to remind us how fortunate we were to
be able to eat whatever we wanted on most days. While eating
only rice was a temporary annoyance for us, it was a luxury for
billions of people around the world who sometimes went to bed
hungry. Whatever our situation, some perspective doesn't hurt.

Where do you rank the world?

The vast majority of Americans are not just doing okay but are
wealthy when compared to the world. Despite a large decrease in
extreme poverty in the world over the last 20 years, there are

billions of people who live on $1 or $2 a day. That means living without electricity or clean water. It also means not eating enough, eating meat maybe once a month if lucky (that 99-cent McDonald's cheeseburger some Americans will not even look at would be an incredibly luxurious meal for much of the world), and perhaps suffering regularly from diarrhea.

The least fortunate 10% of Americans have a higher income than the vast majority of people in China, India, and Brazil. Branko Milanovic's book *The Haves and Have-Nots* shows that in 2010, the poorest 5% of Americans were richer than almost 70% of the world. Yes, China, Brazil, and India's billionaires are richer than almost every individual American. But here is something remarkable:

> The combined income of the poorest 5% of Americans is greater than the combined income of the richest 5% of Indians, including the income of all Indian billionaires.

India is a beautiful country with great potential. But it is still a country where extreme poverty is widespread and few people are middle class. Another way to think about it is that low-income Americans, while struggling and deserving our support, would be considered middle-class or even upper-class in most countries.

There are websites that calculate where you rank in the world based on your income or net worth. Globalrichlist.com, givingwhatwecan.org, and worldwealthcalculator.org are three of them.

Let's go to globalrichlist.com and see where we rank. On this site, we have a choice between typing in how much we make a year after taxes or putting in our net worth (everything we own minus everything we owe). Let's use our income. If I make $8.00 an hour and work 35 hours a week as a cook at a restaurant, I make $280 a week. If I work 50 weeks a year (taking off two weeks for vacation), then I make $14,000 a year before taxes. Let's assume I make about $11,000 after taxes (just a guess, but it will do for us). I select "USA (Dollar)" under "Select location" and type in "11,000."

So where do I stand if I make $11,000 a year after taxes? I am in the top 15% in the world by income. As of July 2016, there are about 7.3 billion people in the world. So I rank about 910 million out of 7.3 billion people. There are 6.4 billion poorer than me when I make $8 an hour.

Some of us will be bothered by the fact that there are almost one billion people who make more money than us. But instead of being embarrassed or angry about our job or pay, we might choose to focus on the fact that flipping burgers for $8 an hour puts us ahead of so many people *before we do anything else.* If you would like to make more money, then you have opportunities to do so. Many restaurants in my area have Help Wanted signs. I spoke to several managers and they said that it is very difficult to find and keep workers. In-N-Out, the California burger chain, offers $12 per hour to start. Or you can enroll in a program to learn a trade like plumbing or carpentry. Where I live there is a plumbing apprentice program that pays you $20 an hour to start as a trainee. Or you could save money and go to school to learn a useful skill. Whatever you want. You have opportunities

If you are curious, you would be in the top 3.7% in the world if you earn $20,000 a year after taxes and the top 0.31% in the world if you make $50,000 a year after taxes.

I am not saying that you should be happy and grateful if you make $15,000, $35,000, $50,000 or any amount in a year. I have no idea what makes you happy. You should do what makes you happy, whether that is making $15,000 a year or $1 million a year. All I am saying is that making minimum wage in America makes us awfully well-off from a global perspective. That knowledge can help us start at the bottom if that is what we must do. It has been said:

> We all live someone else's dream, and dream of someone else's life.

Just by living in America we are living a dream that so many people around the world want:

> "My Lyft driver [from Ukraine] would like to inform me that being stuck in Seattle traffic is 3,000 times better than living in Ukraine." (Tweet by Andrew Maier)

Ukraine is a fine country. But America is so much richer and has so many more opportunities. Andy Warhol uniquely captured one of the special things about America:

> What's great about this country is that America started the tradition where the richest consumers buy essentially

the same things as the poorest. You can be watching TV and see Coca-Cola, and you know that the President drinks Coke, Liz Taylor drinks Coke, and just think, you can drink Coke, too. A Coke is a Coke and no amount of money can get you a better Coke . . . .

If a rich American wants to buy the best milk or orange juice that money can buy, he or she will have to go to the regular grocery store like the person with a minimum-wage job. One way to describe America is a place where anybody can buy most of the highest-quality products by working at a job that anybody can get. And that's just the start.

Chapter 11

Poems

There's no money in poetry,
but there's no poetry in money, either.

Robert Graves

Few things annoyed me more than poems during my school days. Why didn't poets write normally? Why do they get to fill a line with just three words? Or sometimes just a word? What are they saying? Why do they get to break the rules and get famous for making no sense? And the grammar seemed all wrong. So I did not blame myself for not understanding a poem. I suppose not being so hard on myself was not the worst thing in the world.

Occasionally, I would read a poem that captured exactly how I felt with brevity and style. The smart thing to do would have been to look for other interesting poems while ignoring poems that did nothing for me. Instead, I thought I did not have permission to like only what I liked. So I avoided poems for many years. I think many people have this misunderstanding that you must like everything about a subject to have the right to be a fan of it. You can pick and choose. You should seek what inspires you and leave aside the rest.

Here are two poems that I find fun and thoughtful. If you like even a single line, you should explore other poems. I bet you will find one that you end up memorizing because you enjoy reading it again and again.

The first poem is *We Real Cool* by Gwendolyn Brooks. Here are parts of it:

. . .

We real cool. We
Left School. We

Lurk late. We
Strike straight. We

. . .

Jazz June. We
Die soon.

In the poem, some friends are shooting pool after either ditching or dropping out of school. They are hanging out late into the exciting June night. But the night will end, just as the summer—and their lives—will end at some point. The poem takes me back to my school days. I am having fun with my friends. We are laughing and we want the night to last forever. But we know the fun will end. The memories may stay with us, but the memories will only sharpen the pain of knowing that the night is gone forever. Sure, the summer may not be over yet, but it seems that there are only a handful of days and nights when all seem perfect. Children seem to know that there are only a few truly memorable summer nights. Isn't that why they are so reluctant to go home as the sun is setting? They linger and try to make the moment last forever. Of course they fail, as we all fail when we try to preserve a moment.

We Real Cool may have nothing, something, or a lot to do with my reaction to it. Whatever Ms. Brooks intended, I think she would be happy if people read her poem, thought about it, and was changed by it. Poems can have a stylish energy even when delivering sober messages. A poem of ten lines can deliver a knockout truth that a novel might need 300 pages to do.

So is *We Real Cool* a sad poem about how happiness never lasts? Or is it a wakeup call that urges us to seize everyday and make the best of it? Or both? Or none of the above? You decide.

I think one of the things the poem is about is how happiness is not possible without sadness. Would we enjoy as much the time spent with family and friends if we knew that life was forever and that we weren't running out of time? Would we enjoy the time at all? Would that summer night with the cool breeze and exhilarating mood and mysterious possibilities be so thrilling if we knew we had an endless supply of such days?

Consider the movie *Ferris Bueller's Day Off*. It is about high school senior Ferris having a wonderful day with his friends, just like the pool players in *We Real Cool*. Ferris pretends to be sick and so his parents let him skip school. Then he tricks the school dean to letting his girlfriend Sloane leave school early. Then Ferris borrows his best friend Cameron's dad's Ferrari and the three of them have a blast in downtown Chicago: they eat lunch at a fancy restaurant while pretending to be rich and famous, attend an afternoon baseball game, sing and dance in a parade, visit a museum, and relax by the pool. A perfect day.

But would it be special if you ditched school and dragged your friends out of school every day? The thrill of ditching comes from the fact that it almost never happens. Ferris's day off is special because it will probably never happen again. Even if they pull off another ditch day, it won't be the same. The truth is that we get one ditch day.

The passage and urgency of time is everywhere in *Ferris Bueller*. Ferris needs to get his girlfriend out of school before the day drifts into the afternoon—what's the point of ditching school after lunch? Ferris worries that things will change when he goes to college. He vows to see his girlfriend and best buddy during vacations, but he knows that things won't be the same. When he kisses Sloane, he has to race home before his parents return from work. The perfect moment is just a moment.

We don't have forever. Our time is limited. We know these things. But we forget. So art such as *We Real Cool* and *Ferris Bueller* remind us. And not just for kids.

Why are we talking about the movie *Ferris Bueller* in a chapter about poems? Because art is about the universal—things that we all experience. There are countless varieties of art, but they seem to dwell on just a few messages. As I noted in Chapter 3, one of the most memorable lines in *Ferris Bueller* is:

> Life moves pretty fast. If you don't stop and look around once in a while, you could miss it.

Doesn't *We Real Cool* say something similar?
The next poem is *If* by Rudyard Kipling:

If you can keep your head when all about you
    Are losing theirs and blaming it on you,
If you can trust yourself when all men doubt you,
    But make allowance for their doubting too;
If you can wait and not be tired by waiting,
    Or being lied about, don't deal in lies,
Or being hated, don't give way to hating,
    And yet don't look too good, nor talk too wise:

If you can dream - and not make dreams your master;
. . .
If you can meet with Triumph and Disaster
    And treat those two imposters just the same;
. . .
Or watch the things you have your life to, broken,
    And stoop and build'em up with worn-out tools:

If you can make one heap of all your winnings
    And risk it on one turn of pitch-and-toss,
And lose, and start again at your beginning
    And never breathe a word about your loss;
. . .
(emphasis added)

For me, *If* is about being strong against everything that life throws at us with confident modesty and fatalistic optimism. Is this attitude achievable? I'm not sure, but *If* inspires me to try. When words inspire, they have done their job and the rest is up to us.

Note the lines that say, "If you can meet with Triumph and Disaster And treat those two imposters just the same." In other words, success and failure are not what they seem. Then what are they? Recall Chapter 6 where we noted success is failure if we fail to move on, and failure is success if we keep moving. As we have said repeatedly, none of these sayings are new. Many have said it many times many years ago. But the problem is we forget. And inspiring words seem to be one of the few ways to remember and apply what we claim to know. So find and save the words that you find inspiring.

Chapter 12

Maps

There is no special providence for Americans,
and their nature is the same with that of others.

John Adams

In the quote above, one of the Founding Fathers says that Americans are no better than others.

But if Americans are not special, then what explains America's world-changing success? Isn't America great because Americans work hard and are virtuous? No more hard working or virtuous than many others according to America's second president. Then what about this possibility: America is America because of its location. It sounds too simple and obviously wrong. That means we should look into it.

America: best location in the world?

We tend to think about geography as something separate from politics, culture, and the really important things that determine a country's destiny. Geography is boring. Geography is mountains, rivers, deserts, and oceans. It is nice to have a beautiful landscape, but what do rocks and water have to do with a country's economy and politics? Maybe everything. Robert D. Kaplan in his book *The Revenge of Geography* argues that we must recognize and respect the often decisive and always immovable role of geography in shaping history.

When thinking about why America is a wealthy democracy, consider the following facts:

- The Atlantic and Pacific Oceans separate America from the rest of the world.
- America has vast stretches of rich farmland.
- America has a long coastline with many excellent natural harbors facing the open seas.
- America has enormous amounts of natural resources like oil, coal, natural gas, and timber.

What do farmland, oceans, and oil have to do with the America's freedom-loving character and massive wealth? Consider:

- Perhaps the most basic and important geographic fact about the United States is how the Atlantic and Pacific Oceans have protected America from aristocratic and authoritarian enemies for all its history. These massive ocean buffers were especially important during America's first decades as an independent country. If America were in Europe next to Germany, France, or Russia, then there is a good chance that the U.S. would have been invaded and occupied by these powerful countries. The oceans provided peace and stability for democracy to develop in America.

- For much of American history, the average American could go west and own productive farm land. America's rivers, lakes, and seas were full of fish. These factors have made Americans the best fed people for the last 250 years. Also, the open seas and harbors encouraged trade. And where there is trade, there is wealth and a preference for freedom. People want to trade freely with others and make money.

These favorable conditions gave Americans the highest standard of living in the world already by the mid–1700s (of course, we can't say the same thing about enslaved Americans). And being the wealthiest people in the world and not having to worry about foreign invasion are things likely to make any people more optimistic, idealistic, and drawn to freedom and democracy.

In contrast, think about countries where food and resources are scarce and neighbors are hostile. To develop the economy and defend against foreign threats, less geographically fortunate countries needed a strong central government to mobilize their people and resources. The mobilization often involved coercing people to work for collective goals. These countries' priorities were defending against invasion and not starving rather than upholding freedom and democracy. So it is possible that other peoples would have been just as freedom loving as Americans if they had the geographic and material advantages Americans enjoyed. Put bluntly, perhaps Americans are, as John Adams said, just like Germans and Russians, but our rocks and rivers and location are much, much better. Here is Kaplan and others in *The Revenge of Geography*:

> [I]t is geography that has helped sustain American prosperity and which may be ultimately responsible for America's **pan-humanistic altruism.**

> ... America and Britain could **champion freedom because the sea protected them** [from landlocked countries that were often the enemies of liberty.]

> [The Pacific and Atlantic] oceans . . . gave Americans the luxury of their **idealism** . . . . (emphasis added)

As an American, I don't like giving credit to navigable rivers and good dirt for any part of America's success. Such geographic determinism seems to tell Americans that we are just lucky. It downplays or dismisses the idea of America as an unique place and the last best hope for the world.

But understanding America's unique geographic advantages does not mean we have to think lesser of America. Let's say that America has the most geographic advantages of any country in the world. So what? Americans still could have failed. Perhaps it is only because Americans had enough virtue, political wisdom, selfless leaders, work ethic, and a sense of destiny that America became America. And America is not the only country with advantages such as abundant natural resources and geographic protection against foreign enemies. Yet America, despite its faults, has been the difference maker for world freedom. We can be proud of America's accomplishments and also be more appreciative and humble about America's good fortune.

Such a perspective has two benefits. First, if we know that only an once-in-the-history-of-humanity combination of virtue, skill, and luck made America the difference maker for freedom in modern times, then we can appreciate America even more. Second, we can be more understanding of other nations. More empathy for others does not mean we have to compromise America's principles or denigrate its accomplishments. It does mean understanding that there are reasons—very big and immovable reasons such as oceans and mountains—for cultural, economic, and political differences. It is to acknowledge that nations are different because the unforgiving demands of national survival meant freedom, democracy, and optimism were luxuries many could not afford and still cannot afford today.

Russia: worst location in the world?

If the U.S. has one of the best locations in the world, then which country has one of the worst? How about Russia. Russia is the largest country in the world. It is almost twice as large as the U.S. Yet Russia has little natural barriers such as mountains against invasion along its western, southern, and eastern borders. Much of Russia's land borders sit on endlessly flat terrain that stretches the length of the country. Look up the Wikipedia page for "Eurasian Steppe" to get a sense of Russia's geographic vulnerability. (A steppe, pronounced "step," means flat grasslands.)

The U.S. also has vast stretches of flat grasslands: the Great Plains. The Great Plains stretch 2,000 miles up and down through the middle of America, from Montana and North Dakota to Texas. The Great Plains make the U.S. vulnerable to invasion by Canada and Mexico. But Canada and Mexico have never been threats to the U.S. America's most dangerous enemies have always been on the other side of the world, separated by the Atlantic and Pacific Oceans. In contrast, Russia's enemies have always been right on its borders. In terms of geography, Russia is the opposite of the U.S.

Could this opposition explain partly why in the 20th century the two countries threatened each other with total nuclear destruction and why in 2016 they are in many ways still each other's most dangerous political and military rival? Could their stark geographic differences explain why their national characters are so different and why their histories are at opposite ends of the human experience? Americans seem defined by optimism and progress. Russians seem often trapped by unspeakable tragedy and suffering.

Nomadic invaders such as the Huns and Mongols brought incredible destruction to Russia for a thousand years. Some historians believe that these nomadic invasions out of Asia were the most important events that shaped the second millennium. Here is Kaplan in *The Revenge of Geography*:

> [O]ut of the naked southern steppe **from the fifth to the sixteenth centuries came a succession of nomadic invaders**[.] For on the [Russian grasslands] the land is **unceasingly flat**, the climate hard, and the

vegetable production limited to grass, in turn destroyed by sand, driven by powerful winds. Such conditions bred hard and cruel races of men who had at once to destroy any adversaries they came across or be destroyed themselves, as there was no better means of defense in one spot than in another.

Russia . . . fell prey in the thirteenth century to the Golden Horde of the Mongols. Thus[,] . . . Russia [was] **denied access to the European Renaissance,** and **branded forever with the bitterest feelings of inferiority and insecurity**. [W]ith no natural **barriers against invasion** save for the forest itself, Russia would know forevermore what it was like to be **brutally conquered**, and as a result would become perennially obsessed with expanding and holding territory . . . .

[T]he Mongol invasions out of Central Asia **decimated** and subsequently changed not only Russia, but Turkey, Iran, India, China, and the northern reaches of the Arab Middle East . . . . (emphasis added)

Imagine how difficult it is to maintain a stable and free society if a country is regularly invaded and destroyed. When all your resources and energy must be used to just survive and avoid getting massacred, your priority is not democracy and universal rights. When Russia was conquered by the Mongols in the

1200s, Russia missed out on the subsequent European Renaissance that led to the rediscovery and advance in science and culture. Getting left behind contributed to the sense of Russia's "backwardness" that continues to today.

Another reason Russia has never been as wealthy as Western Europe is because Russia is far from the open seas that facilitate trade. You might be confused by the previous sentence because Russia's entire north and east coasts face water. But the north coast faces the Arctic Ocean, which is frozen during parts of the year. Also, northern Russia (called the Extreme North) is sparsely populated and is not close to the commercial centers of Europe and Asia. Russia's east coast is also far from economic centers and has relatively few people. Here is Kaplan discussing the American military strategist Alfred Mahan's analysis of how Russian geography affects the Russian character:

> Russia's **'irremediable remoteness from an open sea** has helped put it in a **disadvantageous position for the accumulation of wealth**[.]' 'This being so, it is natural and proper that [Russia] should be dissatisfied, and dissatisfaction readily takes the form of aggression.' (emphasis added)

Remember how open seas, rivers, and harbors make trade easier, and where there is trade there is wealth.

Of course, Russia is not the only country with geographic disadvantages. For example, France is located next to its historic rival Germany. And this proximity meant France and Germany fought three wars against each other from 1870 to 1945: the

Franco-Prussian War of 1870, World War I from 1914 to 1918, and World War II from 1939 to 1945. In World War I alone, France lost 1.7 million people, or 4.3% of its population at the time. But Russia's wartime losses in the 20th century have been much greater. In World War II, the Soviet Union (Russia) lost 26 million soldiers and civilians out of a total population of 194 million. That is 14% of the population in one war.

To put Russia's losses in World War II in context, imagine America in 2016 losing 14% of its 320 million people. That is 45 million Americans dying in a war against a neighboring country.

Why did the Soviet Union lose so many people? You may not know that there was more fierce fighting between the Soviet Union and Germany in the Eastern Front of World War II than between the Western Allies and Germany in the Western Front. Germany used most of its soldiers and equipment fighting the Soviet Union on the Eastern Front. Germany invaded Russia by driving across Russia's flat and defenseless terrain. The Soviet military and Russian winter eventually defeated the German army, but not before the Soviet Union suffered greatly. Russia's vulnerable geography is not something that was important only 1,000 years ago against the Mongols. Vulnerable geography led to the death of 26 million Russians not too long ago from today's world of smartphones and Pokémon. So when I ask myself why Russian history has been so tragic and violent and why Russia continues its autocratic tradition, I try to remember that the Russian experience has been shaped by its unforgiving geography.

This is not to say that mountains, canyons, rivers, deserts, and oceans determine completely a nation's destiny and all its virtues and faults. The Soviet Union, whatever its origins, was a monstrous tyranny that killed and ruined the lives of tens of millions of people. We can, however, understand and respect geography and the restrictions it places on human dreams. I don't like the idea of predetermined lives. Who does? All of us want to be in control of our destiny. But history tells us that our options are shaped by geography. History also teaches us that tragedy is the norm.

America has also experienced tragedies. But compared to almost every country, American history is more about optimism and freedom. Americans should be proud of their accomplishments and what they stand for. And Americans can also remember that our historically unique accomplishments and national character are due in part to our favorable geography. Americans should do so not to downplay our accomplishments but to remember how rare and precious a force for freedom America is. Perhaps no other country is as geographically blessed as America. Americans used that advantage to preserve freedom around the world. No other country can say that.

Chapter 13
Cereal Boxes

To teach people to read without
teaching them not to
believe everything they read
is only to prepare them
for a new slavery.

Jean Guehenno

An expert is a person who has made all the mistakes that
can be made in a very narrow field.

Niels Bohr

It seems to make sense: eating fat makes us fat and unhealthy because fat is fat—therefore we should avoid or eat less fat. So then we eat a lot of foods with nutrition labels like the following:

Calories	150
Calories from Fat	0

Total Fat	0 g
Total Carbohydrate	27 g
Sugars	23 g

A typical sugary cereal with no fat has this kind of nutrition label. A can of soda has 30 to 40 grams of sugar and no fat.

But what if we got it all wrong? What if there is no scientific evidence showing a link between eating fat and bad health? What if it is the sugar in cereals, bread, pasta, snacks, and soda that makes us overweight and unhealthy? What if we just are not sure about what is good and what is bad for us? These are some of the questions asked by Gary Taubes in "What If It's All Been a Big Fat Lie?" in the July 2002 issue of the *New York Times Magazine*.

In the 1970s, doctors and scientists warned that dietary fat increased the risk of heart diseases. They urged Americans to eat less fatty foods like red meat, whole milk, eggs, and butter. And Americans did just that starting in the 1980s. Food companies also introduced fat-free yogurts, drinks, margarine, sodas, and snacks. Americans saw fat as the enemy while fat-free food was to be enjoyed without worry. So we ate a lot of food with nutrition labels like the ones above: no fat and a lot of sugar.

Some disagreed with the low-fat-is-good-for-everyone advice. Perhaps the most famous dissenter was Dr. Robert Atkins. Atkins said that people could lose weight by eating fat-rich foods like butter, meat, and eggs while avoiding carbohydrates (sugar) because it was the sugar in foods like pasta and bread that caused weight gain, obesity, and heart diseases. Most doctors and scientists dismissed Atkins's idea.

Today, 30 years after Americans started to eat more bread, pasta, and other carbohydrate-heavy foods, more Americans are fatter and sicker than ever. And now more and more doctors and researchers are saying that the less-fat-is-better advice not only lacked scientific proof but may have caused the obesity crisis. Before we go on, let me say that you should not take anything in this chapter as medical advice. But even if we are not doctors, we can use common sense to evaluate the claims of experts.

Here are some facts about Americans' health:

- In 2012, about 35% of American adults were obese and another 30% were overweight. So two-thirds of American adults are obese or overweight. Overweight means you weigh more than recommended. Obese means you weigh even more than an overweight person. For every 100 Americans, only about 33 Americans have somewhere around the recommended weight. (About 2% of Americans are underweight.)

- 1 out of every 3 children and adolescents aged six to 19 are either overweight or obese. Almost 20% of kids aged six to 19 are obese.

The rise of obesity is recent. The obesity rate stayed around 14% through the 1960s and 1970s. The rate shot up in the 1980s and by the late 1980s almost 25% of Americans were obese. This trend continued in the 1990s and 2000s and now 35% of American adults are obese and another 30% are overweight.

As we noted, one thing that changed in the 1980s and 1990s was that Americans started to eat more sugar-heavy foods like sodas, cookies and chips, cereals, and bread due in part to researchers urging Americans to eat less fat. To understand why health experts spread the anti-fat message, we need to go back to January 1961 when physiologist Ancel Keys was on the cover of *Time* magazine. Keys argued that dietary fat causes heart disease by raising the cholesterol level. Keys's fat-causes-heart-disease argument was based on a study that is now criticized for handpicking only the data that supported Keys's hypothesis and ignoring opposing data. In 1961, Keys's idea was a big deal that seemed to deserve attention, especially since a respected magazine like *Time* put Keys on its cover.

But, Gary Taubes says:

> . . . Keys . . . introduced the low-fat-is-good-health dogma in the [1950s]. . . . Over the next [20 years], however, the **scientific evidence supporting this theory remained stubbornly ambiguous**. (emphasis added)

So there was no clear evidence to support Keys's idea that a high-fat diet was unhealthy or that a low-fat diet was healthy. Then why did doctors and journalists urge Americans to change to a low-fat diet? Here is Taubes's answer:

> The [question over Keys's theory that low-fat is good for health] was eventually settled not by new science but by politics.

Taubes writes that from 1977 to 1984, the National Institutes of Health spent

> several hundred million dollars trying to demonstrate a connection between **eating fat and getting heart disease** and, despite what we might think, it **failed**. Five major studies revealed **no such link**. (emphasis added)

There was a sixth study, and this study found that a group of people who were given a cholesterol-lowering drug had a lower death rate from heart diseases. Here are the facts of the experiment as summarized by Tom Naughton on his blog Fathead-movie.com:

- Over 10 years, 1940 men between the ages 35 and 59 were given daily a cholesterol-reducing drug. Another 1866 men between the ages 35 and 59 were given a placebo (something that has no effect on the body).

Here were the results:

- Among the 1940 men who took the cholesterol-reducing drug, 130 suffered a heart attack, 30 died from heart attacks, and 68 people died from all causes. Among the 1866 men who did not take the drug, 158 suffered a heart attack, 38 died from heart attacks, and 71 people died from all causes.

These results led *Time* magazine in March 1984 to announce that foods high in fat and cholesterol are harmful. Do a web search for "Time cholesterol cover 1984" and you will see two eggs and a bacon making a sad face on the front cover of *Time.*

For centuries, Americans had been enjoying their eggs, butter, whole milk, bacon, and steak—symbols of American prosperity and abundance. Then Americans are told by *Time* (arguably America's most respected current events magazine in the 1980s and even today), newspapers, and experts that they had a higher chance of dying from heart diseases if they continued eat such fatty foods.

Did the sixth study justify this conclusion? Out of the 1940 men who took the pill that lowered their cholesterol, 30 men died from heart attacks. That is a heart-attack death rate of 1.5%. Out of the 1866 men who did not take the cholesterol-lowering pill, 38 died from heart attacks. That is a 2% death rate from heart attacks. The difference between the two groups is 0.5%. The result was interesting and a reason for more studies. But I don't think it called for definitive and sweeping warnings about the dangers of eating eggs, butter, and whole milk. Of course you should make up your own mind after speaking with a doctor.

There is another way to look at the results. The difference between 2% and 1.5% is a half percent when we subtract. But the difference is much greater if we divide. Here's why. Those who did not take the cholesterol-lowering drug had a 2% death rate from heart attacks. Those who did take the drug had a 1.5% death rate. The difference is 0.5% in absolute terms but 25% in percentage terms. Going from 2% to 1.5% is a 25% reduction because 0.5 is 25% of 2. And that is how many people described the results, that those who took the cholesterol lowering drug had a 25% lower death rate than those who did not. This interpretation of the study is not incorrect. But I don't think it's the entire truth because there were five other studies that showed no link between eating fat and getting heart attacks.

Also remember that the sixth study was about the effects of taking a cholesterol-lowering drug, not whether a low-fat diet prevents heart disease. But the thinking behind urging people to eat less fat was that:

> if a cholesterol-lowering drug could prevent heart attacks, then a low-fat, cholesterol-lowering diet **should** do the same. (emphasis added)

The key word is "should." The supervisor of these studies, Basil Rifkind, said:

> It's an imperfect world . . . . The data that would be definitive is ungettable, so you do your best with what is available.

Taubes writes:

> Some of the best scientists disagreed with this low-fat logic, suggesting that good science was incompatible with such **leaps of faith**, but they were effectively ignored. (emphasis added)

For example, cholesterol researcher Pete Ahrens testified in a U.S. Senate hearing that:

[E]veryone responds differently to low-fat diets.

And:

> What right has the federal government to propose that the American people conduct a **vast nutritional experiment**, with themselves as subjects, **on the strength of so very little evidence that it will do them any good?** (emphasis added)

Despite Ahrens's warning that there was no scientific evidence showing who might benefit from a low-fat diet,

> [I]n 1977, . . . a Senate committee . . . published its 'Dietary Goals for the United States,' advising that Americans significantly curb their fat intake to abate an epidemic of 'killer diseases' supposedly sweeping the country.

Also:

> [I]n . . . 1984, . . . the National Institutes of Health officially recommend that all Americans over the age of 2 eat less fat.

I am not saying you should eat bacon and eggs every day. I am not saying you should stop eating bread and pasta. I am not saying you have to eat butter. I am not saying anything about what anyone should or should not eat. I am saying that an increasing number of doctors and scientists are saying that there was no strong evidence showing that eating less fat-rich foods would make Americans healthier. Recent studies also do not show a connection between butter and heart disease. So who is right? After all that we have learned about the fallibility of experts, I think the only reasonable response is: we don't know. The problem is that we want perfect answers about something that is one of the most mysterious things in the universe: the human body. While modern medicine saves many lives, there is still much we don't know about ourselves. Given this uncertainty plus differences among people, it seems caution is appropriate regarding sweeping advice about diet.

What We Can Do

Consider the following facts from Daniel Akst's book *We Have Met the Enemy*:

- Smoking causes over 450,000 deaths a year.
- About 800,000 Americans die prematurely every year from "just three behaviors: smoking, inactivity, and a lousy diet."

In comparison, 400,000 Americans were killed in World War II from 1941 to 1945. We think of World War II as perhaps the greatest tragedy in history. Yet we have a somewhat casual attitude about smoking, not exercising, and eating too much. Common sense suggests we can prevent many premature deaths by not eating too much, not smoking, and not sitting all day.

I learned in *We Have Met the Enemy* that there are about 220,000 weight-loss surgeries done in America every year. These involve blocking "off parts of the stomach or removing some intestine." Before we get judgmental, let's remember that some people are born larger than others. Some are born healthier than others. Some gain weight easily while others have a hard time gaining weight. We are all different, and we have different strengths and weaknesses. That said, remember that the obesity rate in America held steady at around 14% before surging to 35% in recent years. Bad or incomplete health advice likely played some role. But what about ourselves? Akst writes the following about talking to a nurse at a weight-loss surgery conference (remember, self-improvement—not rudeness—is the goal):

> The nurse was extremely [overweight] despite having had [weight-loss] surgery herself, and she contended that self-control was not the issue: people's weight problems are genetic, or the result of high-fructose corn syrup, or fast food, or ignorance of healthy eating, or advertising, or their inability to access or afford fruits and vegetables. And while this prosperous, well-educated health care professional made these arguments—all of which have some plausible basis in fact—she ate not one but two Styrofoam plates full of waffles, smeared heavily with cream cheese.

We don't know everything about the human body, but we do know that eating too much is not good for us. And we must believe that we have some control over how much we eat. Eating two plates of waffles soaked in syrup once in a while will not kill us, but eating that much of that kind of food often is probably not a healthy thing. We don't need experts to tell us that.

Chapter 14
Bad Words

Under certain circumstances, profanity provides
a relief denied even to prayer.

Mark Twain

Of what use is freedom of speech
to those who fear to offend?

Roger Ebert

Why do workers at a construction site tend to have a "rougher" way
of talking than office workers? We all use bad words sometimes, but
those who work with their hands seem to generally have a more direct
way of speaking. When my neighbor got a new roof, I watched the
crew members work. When they talked, the talking was more
commanding and yelling than asking and saying "please."

Why might roofers, carpenters, electricians, plumbers, and
others in the trades talk differently than lawyers or accountants?
Could it be that plumbers, electricians, carpenters, and others on
a job site talk like they do because they *can* talk that way? As

Matthew Crawford says in his book *Shop Class as Soulcraft: An Inquiry into the Value of Work*:

> There is a **real freedom of speech** on a [construction or project] site [as opposed to an office job.] (emphasis added)

You can't swear or say controversial things in an office. You could, but you'll get in trouble. I'm sure many people pretend to agree with whatever seems to be the popular opinion among their colleagues. There are speech codes in an office. Why? One reason seems well-intentioned enough: people want to get along and get some work done by not saying offensive things to each other.

But Matthew Crawford suggests another reason why you don't have freedom of speech in the office. In most of the work done in large companies:

> one's work is meaningless taken by itself.

For example, an office worker might write the first draft or a section of a report, but the final version is completed after five or eight or even dozens of people work on it. Few people can identify their individual contribution to the final product. So it is difficult judge an employee's work performance. The result is that your job security depends:

> entirely on . . . personal relationships, in part because the **criteria of evaluation are ambiguous**. (emphasis added)

And when your job security depends on personal relationships, you have to be very careful about what you say in the workplace.

So why do plumbers and electricians get to, in Crawford's words, "tell dirty jokes"? Crawford says that working on a job site means that you do work that can be judged for its quality and worth. You either did a good job wiring the house or you did a lousy job. You either installed the plumbing correctly or you did not. You either built the house frame properly or you did not. Working on a job site means that you have your own project and you either do it well or you suck. So if you wired the house correctly, installed the pipes correctly, or framed the house correctly, then

> you have grounds for knowing your own work independently of others, and it is the same grounds on which others will make *their* judgments.

In other words, if you do your task well, you have good reasons to be proud and for others to respect you as a skilled worker. And so Crawford says:

> there is **less reason to manage appearances**. There is **real freedom of speech on a job site**, which reverberates outward and **sustains a wider liberality**. You can tell dirty jokes. Where there is real work being done, the order of things isn't quite so fragile. (emphasis added)

Crawford is not glorifying the freedom to tell crude jokes. He is saying that there are deeply meaningful benefits to doing work that can be judged for its quality and worth every day—and the ability to swear is just a side effect of the freedom in a job site. In turn, the "polite" speech in office jobs may reflect necessary collective deception rather than simply good-heartedness.

Again, what's at stake goes beyond using profanity. There are real spiritual and material benefits to making a living by fixing and making things with your hands. But the current focus on pushing everyone to attend college discourages people from exploring different career paths and choosing a vocation that fits their personality and interest. Not only do many carpenters, plumbers, electricians, mechanics, machine operators, and others with dirty hands at the end of the workday often make more money than office workers, they may enjoy a sense of accomplishment from their work that eludes many with "prestigious" office jobs. If you don't want to or didn't go to college and are looking for something to do, try working with your hands and see if you like it.

Few things are as they seem. We should remember this the next time we see men and women working at a job site.

Chapter 15
Sad Words

It doesn't hurt to feel sad from time to time.

Willie Nelson

Do you not see how necessary a world of pains and troubles is
to school an intelligence and make it a soul?

John Keats

Can sadness ever be good? How do we start talking about a topic
as wide, mysterious, and sad as sadness? Let's narrow our topic a
bit. We are not talking about mental illnesses that can torture the
mind and body to the point of self-destruction and require
medical help. We are also not talking about having a bad day at
work or our sports team losing. We are left with everything in
between, including feeling melancholy to grieving over the death
of a family member.

While we should not want to be sad every day, it seems that
overcoming disappointments and frustrations can make us

stronger, more aware, and more balanced. Maybe even more humble. So yes, sadness—or more accurately, our sturdy and reflective response to trouble—can be good.

But I think there is a more fundamental and interesting question than whether sadness is good or bad. The better question is how we might use the inevitable sadness to make our lives better since all of us will experience deep sadness at least a few times in our life.

The worst thing we can do is try to avoid sadness at all cost. Avoidance is an understandable wish. Who wants to deal with crushing disappointments and heartbreaks? But trying to avoid the unavoidable means we come to *fear* sadness. And fear is self-destruction. None other than *Star Wars*' Yoda said so:

> Fear is the path to the dark side. Fear leads to anger.
> Anger leads to hate. Hate leads to suffering.

There are many causes of sadness, but sadness over time's exasperatingly relentless march forward must be the most basic. Everything and everyone we love will disappear, at least in the physical world. Eric G. Wilson writes in his 2008 *Los Angeles Times* essay "The Miracle of Melancholia" that the poet John Keats said:

> "melancholy . . . is our awareness of things inevitably passing—of brothers dying before they reach 20; of nightingales that cease their songs; of [flowers] drooping at noon."

How can we deal with the inevitable end of everything? Let's discuss two ways.

Detachment

One strategy—Yoda's strategy—is to not care so much. Cass Sunstein wrote about his interpretation of the *Star Wars* movies in an essay titled "I Am You Father" in the May 2016 issue of *The Atlantic* magazine. Sunstein writes that Buddhism, Stoicism, and Yoda urge us to be detached and to "let go" because if "you are attached to someone, you become vulnerable." That's true. Loving anyone or anything means we fear losing it. And fear—if you believe Yoda, as I do—can lead to bad things. Love really is dangerous.

You may know that in the *Star Wars* movies, Anakin Skywalker turns to the Dark Side and becomes the evil Darth Vader because he desperately wants the power to save the lives of those he loves. Yoda warned Anakin about this temptation because Yoda knew the dangers of passion and attachment. Sunstein writes that Yoda urged Anakin, "Train yourself to let go of everything you fear to lose." Yoda said, "Let go of fear, and loss cannot harm you." Similarly, the Stoics said that we should never mourn. Of course Anakin mourns and cannot let go and ruins the galaxy for everyone.

But can we blame Anakin for turning to the Dark Side? I'm not sure we would do better. If you were promised the power to prevent a loved from dying, wouldn't you be at least tempted to put on a mask and call yourself Darth Something? This temptation points to the difficulty of detachment. It seems impossible not to mourn.

Of course, we do move on from loss. So in a sense we eventually let go and reach some kind of detachment. But the Stoics and Yoda seem to demand more than just moving on *after* loss. They seem to say we should move on and let go *before* the loss. While they do not say that we should turn our backs on our family and friends while they are alive, they seem to require us to maintain *some* emotional distance from loved ones. But then don't they cease to be loved ones?

Embracing Obsession and Crushes

If detachment seems too strict, aloof, and cold-hearted, then let's discuss another option. What about maximum attachment, passion, and possession? Grab onto friends and family as tight as we can while we have time. The Stoics and Yoda would say that a passionate approach to life is risky: look how the innocent and well-meaning Anakin became Darth Vader because he loved his family so much. It is difficult to move on from intense attachments. Our sadness will be deeper and perhaps debilitating.

Despite these disadvantages, I can think of three reasons why someone might prefer a life of intense attachments and even obsessions over a life of staying at a distance.

The first reason is that not caring so much about our family and friends just isn't possible for many of us. And if aloofness cannot be achieved, then we might as well love "too much." Enjoy now and deal with the consequences later.

Second, love makes us vulnerable, but love also creates memories, and memories are important. Memories keep us going by reminding us that we can again be the best version of ourselves. A character in Haruki Murakami's novel *After Dark* says:

> [P]eople's memories are maybe the fuel they burn to
> stay alive. Whether those memories have any actual

importance or not, it doesn't matter as far as the maintenance of life is concerned.

Third, although we get sad about the "inevitabl[e] passing" of things we love, Wilson says it is:

> precisely when we sense impending death that we grasp the world's beauty.

Death creates urgency, and urgency is not a bad thing. Wilson says death can:

> reconcile us to facts, no matter how harsh, and that also can inspire us to imagine new and more creative ways to engage with the world.

With time running out, there is a better chance that we get busy living, trying different things, caring more, loving more, forgiving sooner, finishing a project, or creating something.

I think the most important thing about sadness is that it is okay to be sad. I agree with Wilson who says:

> Melancholia, far from error or defect, is an almost miraculous invitation to rise above the contented status quo and imagine untapped possibilities.

While we cannot avoid sadness, we can be encouraged in knowing that it may lead to some of our greatest victories.

Chapter 16
Electronic Words

The real problem is not whether machines think
but whether men do.

B.F. Skinner

As I emphasized at the beginning, I do not believe in a list of "serious" books that are the only places to find perspective, fun, and wisdom. I have always found essays and other short pieces to be as life-changing and enjoyable as my favorite books. And the number of books we read is unimportant. Reviewing now and then a few of our favorites can make all the difference. You should read whatever catches your imagination and ignore everyone and everything else.

One source you might not think of as reading is Twitter. On Twitter, I follow those who provide funny, provocative, comforting, and sometimes infuriating views on various topics. I find Twitter to be a useful tool to find new ideas and relearn old lessons.

I have two suggestions for Twitter. First, don't stare at your Twitter feed all day. Words are just words. We have to apply what we know in the real world—and we already know a lot. Second, be open to different views. I do not follow those who I find unnecessarily harsh, but I try to follow those whose opinions challenge me.

I find valuable Twitter's stream of reminders about values I believe in and try to live up to. That said, let's remember our discussion about the limits of technology from Chapter 3. Twitter and the Internet can be useful and even transformative. But I think it is healthy to remember that we can—and in many ways we must—grow and learn without technology. Technology can add to our self-education, but technology cannot supply the discipline and patience. It is convenient to find and store ideas on Twitter, but I can always look up a book or magazine and use pencil and paper instead. The Internet can be incredible, but there is always the library. Remember that we have in ourselves everything we need.

Chapter 17

Just A Few Words

Resolve to [get] in a little reading every day,
if it is but a single sentence.

Horace Mann

People more often need to be reminded than informed.

Samuel Johnson

Now and then all of us will feel defeated, when it seems no one can or will help us. When it seems impossible to make something out of nothing, we might try remembering simple truths and being open to new ideas. Just a few words can remind us that life is for exploring, that comfort is not always happiness, and that we can again be the best version of ourselves. We know this. We just have to be reminded from time to time.

About the Author

Brian is a teacher, academic consultant, and writer. He has many years of experience helping students of all ages and backgrounds pursue their curiosities and discover new interests. Brian is the author of three books and his articles have appeared in the *Harvard Journal on Legislation*.

Brian studied at Harvard Law School and at the University of California at Berkeley and was a Harvard Law School Post-Graduate Research Fellow. His interests include bicycling and following the financial markets.

You can follow Brian on Twitter @briankimmer and he welcomes comments and hellos at brian.b.kim@gmail.com.